THE ARMY

THE ARMY

"This We'll Defend"

JEREMY P. MAXWELL

amber
BOOKS

Published by Amber Books Ltd
United House
North Road
London N7 9DP
United Kingdom
www.amberbooks.co.uk
Instagram: amberbooksltd
Facebook: amberbooks
Twitter: @amberbooks
Pinterest: amberbooksltd

ISBN: 978-1-83886-061-5

Project Editor: Michael Spilling
Designer: Mark Batley
Picture Research: Terry Forshaw

Printed in China

Contents

The Modern Soldier

In the complex modern world, Army soldiers have to prepare for major conventional threats in large-scale combat operations, as well as maintain and train for counterinsurgency fights that characterized the Cold War period and current operations in the Middle East. The modern American soldier is part of a vast and complex machine that brings together multidomain operations—including the modern advents of cyber and space capabilities—to maintain its status as the most advanced fighting force in the world. Each Army soldier is a master of the skills required by their respective branch. Each soldier must prove their worth and demonstrate that they add value to the needs of the Army.

The modern soldier is part of an integrated environment. The Army is comprised of soldiers from all cultural and social backgrounds found within the United States and its territories, and must be able to work with people from different countries, whether they be part of coalition forces or civilians. The Army is also often required to bring humanitarian relief and medical aid to regions hit by natural disasters and war.

To ensure success in operations that encircle the globe, soldiers must undergo constant training to hone their skills. Training starts at bootcamp or officer training school, where soldiers are indoctrinated into Army culture and customs. Initial training provides the framework—a baseline test of physical stamina and weapons proficiency. However, training is a constant part of Army life. Once newly minted and with their respective branches, soldiers continue to train for the battle that is always looming on the horizon.

OPPOSITE:

Airborne Proficiency Jump, Grafenwoehr Training Area, Germany
Paratroopers assigned to the 173rd Airborne Brigade perform an airborne proficiency jump over Bunker Drop Zone in Grafenwoehr Training Area. Here, members walk out in full jump gear to load on to the descending CH-47 Chinook, a dual-prop helicopter with a range of 200 nautical miles (300 km) that can carry up to 55 troops or 12 tons of cargo.

LEFT:

Honor Guard, Fort Myer, Virginia

Members of the Honor Guard practice their routine so that they work in unison in preparation for the U.S. Army Chief of Staff change of responsibility ceremony at Fort Myer, Virginia. In 2007, General George W. Casey took over as Chief of Staff from General Peter J. Schoomaker in a ceremony hosted by Acting Secretary of the Army Pete Geren.

RIGHT:

158th Aviation Regiment, Task Force 38, Iraq

Spc. Crisma Albarran detaches an ammunition case from its mount after a UH-60 Black Hawk helicopter flight over Iraq, March 2010. Albarran was with Task Force 38's B Company, 3rd Battalion, 158th Aviation Regiment. The 7.62mm ammunition pictured here is attached to the door-mounted M60D machine guns that the Black Hawk can be fitted with.

LEFT TOP:

2nd Cavalry Regiment, Rose Barracks, Germany
Leaders with 2nd Cavalry Regiment run at the front of a regimental formation during a run, 2013. Troops with the regiment ran three miles (5km) during morning physical fitness as a morale booster. In the following months, the 2nd Calvary would deploy to the Kandahar province of Afghanistan for the second time.

LEFT BOTTOM:

Phase I Officer Candidate School, Fort Benning, Ga.
Officer candidates participate in a tug-of-war competition as part of a team-building and physical training session. This exercise, like the many others that take place during initial training, are designed to get recruits into the mindset of team before self.

RIGHT:

Rehabilitation
Army Captain Alex Wilson participates in an archery tournament in Tampa, Florida, during the 2019 Department of Defense Warrior Games. Attended by approximately 300 soldiers, the Warrior Games is an adaptive sports competition for wounded, ill, and injured service members and veterans.

RIGHT:

3rd Infantry Regiment, Inauguration Parade, 2013
Soldiers from the 3rd Infantry Regiment "The Old Guard" participate in the presidential inauguration parade in Washington, D.C., along Pennsylvania Avenue, from the U.S. Capitol to the White House. "The Old Guard" is the oldest active-duty infantry unit in the Army, serving the nation since 1784. It is the Army's official ceremonial unit and escort to the president, and it also provides security for Washington, D.C., in times of national emergency or civil disturbance.

OVERLEAF:

Clearing Mission, Iraq
Army Spc. Steven Robinson and his patrol explosive detection dog, Kay, from the 25th Infantry Division, search a dwelling during a combined clearing mission with Iraqi soldiers in Diyala province.

OPPOSITE LEFT:

Military Working Dog, Jani Khel District, Afghanistan

Nina and her handler, from 3rd Battalion (Airborne), 509th Infantry Regiment, Task Force Gold Geronimo, patrol during Operation Marble Lion in 2012.

OPPOSITE RIGHT TOP:

Combined Joint Task Force, East Africa

Army Private Alexander Hering, from the 2nd Battalion, 506th Infantry Regiment, 101st Airborne Division (Air Assault), secures a perimeter fence with concertina wire. In 2020, soldiers from the 101st were assigned to the East Africa Response Force, providing the ability to rapidly deploy throughout the Indian Ocean.

OPPOSITE RIGHT BOTTOM:

Firefighting Training, 555th Engineer Brigade

Members of the 407th Expeditionary Civil Engineer Squadron undergo fire safety training. The fire department offers classes to Army units to ensure that they are well trained in putting out mine-resistant ambush protective vehicle fires during convoy operations in Iraq.

Truck Rodeo

Spc. Laashton Elliot, a truck driver with the 781st Transportation Company, drills wheel nuggets during a truck rodeo at Kandahar Airfield. The rodeo is an opportunity for truck drivers to sharpen their skills through a series of obstacles to compete for the right to be called "Best Trucking Company on KAF."

Aid Work, Hurricane Sandy, October 2012

The National Guard perform a number of functions, including responding to national emergencies. Here, soldiers from the 50th Infantry Brigade Combat Team, New Jersey Army National Guard, mobilized for Hurricane Sandy, provide assistance to displaced residents at an emergency shelter at the Werblin Recreation Center, Piscataway Township, N.J.

Weapons Training

A Special Operations Forces soldier assigned to 10th Special Forces Group (Airborne) fires during a close range weapons training exercise. Such exercises are part of the training regimen the Army employs to adapt weapon training strategies in a variety of contexts.

Army Crawl, Schofield Barracks, Hawaii

Captain Jasmin Cho, a Pacific North Asia Desk Officer, low crawls with a weapon at the East Range Obstacle Course. The point of the low crawl is to train soldiers to inherently present a small profile and duck beneath enemy fire.

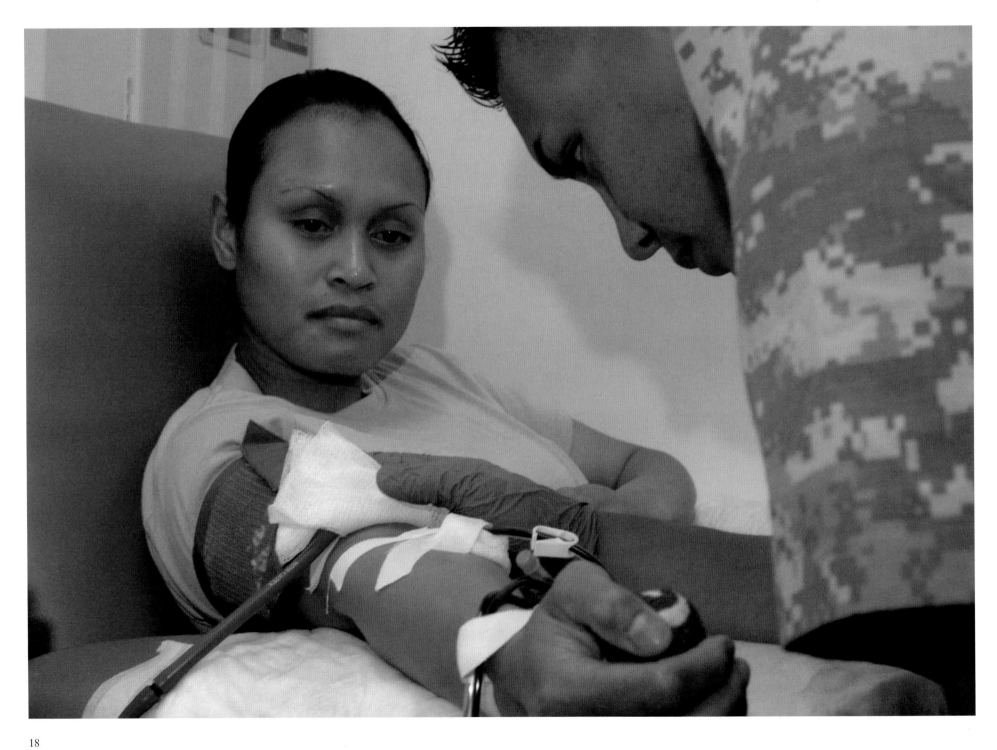

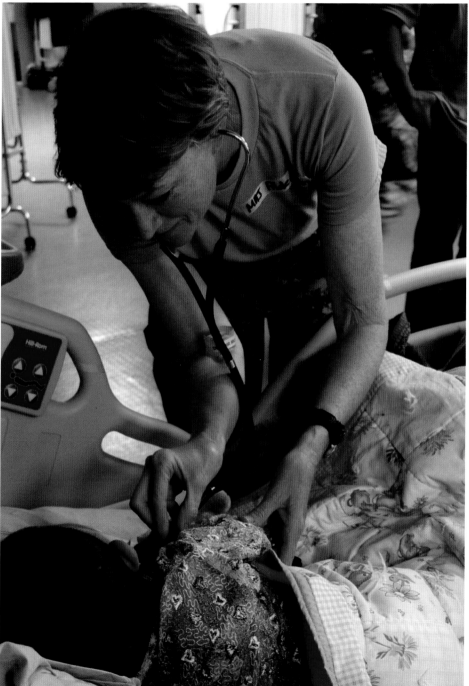

OPPOSITE:
Blood Support Detachment
Army Corporal Christopher LeRoy of the 932nd Blood Support Detachment, monitors the progress of Sergeant Jennifer Skebong, of the 583rd Medlog Company, as she gives blood at Bagram Airfield, Afghanistan.

ABOVE:
Face Camouflage
Soldiers from the 554th Civil Engineering Squadron apply facial camouflage. The unit is participating in a joint Red Horse Team mobility training exercise. Red Horse Teams are highly mobile engineering units from the Army and Air Force that parachute in to seize an airfield, repair it, and make it operational.

RIGHT:
Army Nurse
Army Major Una Alderman, the chief nurse officer for the 452nd Army Reserve, tends to a patient at the hospital on Forward Operating Base Salerno. Salerno is located in the southeastern province of Khost, Afghanistan.

19

LEFT:

M88 Recovery Vehicle
Army Sergeant Jasmine Jenkins, an M88 Recovery Vehicle commander, communicates via radio while on the gun range at the Seventh Army Training Command's Grafenwoehr Training Area, Germany, 2020. The M88 is a fully-tracked armored vehicle used to perform battlefield rescue and recovery missions.

OPPOSITE:

Best Warrior Competition
Army Sergeant Larry J. Isbell, representing the National Guard, watches his firing lane for targets during the M4 Range Qualification event during the Department of the Army's 10th annual Best Warrior Competition. In Army marksmanship training, the minimum score to pass is 23 hits out of 40. Soldiers must hit 23 to 29 targets for a Marksman rating; 30 to 35 for Sharpshooter; and 36 to 40 for an Expert rating.

ABOVE:

Purple Heart Ceremony, Warrior and Family Support Center (WFSC), Joint Base San Antonio-Fort Sam Houston, Texas
Deputy Defense Secretary Ash Carter pins a Purple Heart medal on Army Staff Sergeant Jerry M. Amis during a Purple Heart ceremony as Amis' wife, Nerrisha, looks on. Amis was injured in 2013 when his vehicle was struck by an improvised explosive device (IED) while on mounted patrol in Afghanistan.

RIGHT:

Hat Toss
At the command of "Class dismissed," a class takes part in the longstanding traditional Hat Toss at Michie Stadium, U.S. Military Academy, West Point, New York. Throwing the white hat symbolizes a cadet leaving the cadet life behind and exchanging his cadet hat for a green hat, which marks the start of an Army career.

Origins
to World War I

The American soldier has meant different things over time. When the United States was in its infancy, the militia defended settlements from Native Americans. In the Revolutionary War (1775–1783), the militia joined with the Continental Army to fight the British, who sought to exert their authority over the colonies. In the wake of the Revolutionary War, the U.S. Army was used to expand the new republic westwards. Eventually, their duties extended beyond the confines of the western territories to Mexico. After success in the Mexican–American War (1846–48), the Civil War (1861–65) tore the very fabric of American society apart.

In the wake of the Civil War, the Unites States of America became a true nation, with one concerted focus. With sectional conflict behind them, the U.S. Army moved westward to quash Native American uprisings and exert control over the country's coasts. That would remain their policy until the latter stages of the 19th century, when the Spanish–American War (1898) erupted. That war would forever change the focus of the Army. No longer were they concerned with simply guaranteeing the integrity of America's borders. Protecting the western hemisphere from European colonialism was the initial goal in the Spanish–American War, but it ended in the U.S. acquiring overseas territories in the Philippines, ushering the country—and the U.S. Army—on to the international stage.

The Army played a major part in the later stages of World War I, a global war where the ramifications of imperialism came to a head. Under President Woodrow Wilson and General John Pershing, the American Expeditionary Force was born. It deployed in 1917 and was pivotal in ending a war that had ravaged the world for four years.

OPPOSITE:
Battle of Lexington, April 19, 1775
Lexington was one of three battles that signaled the start of the American Revolutionary War. The British Army set out from Boston to capture rebel leaders Samuel Adams and John Hancock in Lexington, as well as to destroy the Americans' store of weapons and ammunition in nearby Concord.

LEFT:

Siege of Yorktown, September 28–October 19, 1781

The Siege of Yorktown was a decisive victory by a combined force of American Continental Army troops led by General George Washington and French soldiers led by the Comte de Rochambeau over a British force commanded by Lieutenant General Charles Cornwallis. The siege proved to be the last major land battle of the American Revolutionary War, as the surrender by Cornwallis, and the capture of both him and his army, prompted the British government to negotiate an end to the conflict.

RIGHT:

Continental Soldiers

Revolutionary War uniforms varied greatly. Early in the war, many American soldiers wore long brown coats. Starting in 1779, George Washington ordered that uniforms for soldiers in the Continental Army consist of blue coats, white waistcoats, and facings of varying colors. Each state regiment had different colors for the linings, buttons, and facings.

LEFT:

Battle of Chippawa, War of 1812
Lieutenant Colonel James Miller, commander of the 21st Infantry, leads the charge to capture British artillery. The Battle of Chippawa in July 1814 provided a great boost to American morale by demonstrating that the U.S. Army could tangle with British regulars and best them.

ABOVE:

Battle near New Orleans, January 8, 1815
This battle was significant because it thwarted a British effort to gain control of a critical American port and elevated Major General Andrew Jackson to national fame. The battle did not affect the course of the war or the peace negotiations; however, it boosted American

self-confidence, opened the door to territorial expansion, shaped the political landscape until the Civil War, and marked the birth of the American military establishment.

OVERLEAF:

Union Forces, Richmond–Petersburg Campaign, 1865
The Richmond–Petersburg campaign was a series of battles around Petersburg, Virginia, fought from June 15, 1864 to April 2, 1865. The campaign consisted of nine months of trench warfare in which Union forces commanded by

Lieutenant General Ulysses S. Grant assaulted Petersburg unsuccessfully and then constructed trench lines. It was a change from the classic military siege, in which a city is usually surrounded and all supply lines are cut off.

OPPOSITE LEFT:

Flag of the 37th Infantry, 8th Reserves, Pennsylvania Infantry

The regiment was formed in June 1861, and its first state color was received on September 10, 1861. The regiment was composed of men from Armstrong, Butler, Allegheny, Fayette, Philadelphia, Bedford, Clarion, Greene, and Washington counties. The 37th was mustered out of service on May 24, 1864.

OPPOSITE RIGHT TOP:

Federal Artillery Conduct a Crossing on a Raft

A river crossing is a unique operation. It requires specific procedures for success because the water obstacle prevents normal ground maneuver. The nature and size of the obstacle, the enemy situation, and available assets limit the tactical commander's options.

OPPOSITE RIGHT BOTTOM:

Wounded Zouave

The Zouaves were a class of light infantry of the French Army serving between 1830 and 1962 and associated with French North Africa. Numerous Zouave regiments were organized in America, who adopted the name and the North African–inspired uniforms during the Civil War. The Union army deployed more than 70 volunteer Zouave regiments, while the Confederates fielded 25 Zouave companies.

PREVIOUS PAGES:

**Native Americans,
U.S. Cavalry, 1891**
Lakota Sioux, (Oglala)
Company B, United States
Cavalry, pose with their
commander Lieutenant John
J. Pershing, several months
after the Wounded Knee
Massacre in 1891. The Army
Reorganization Act of 1866
authorized the president to
enlist and employ a force
of Native Americans not to
exceed 1000 to act as scouts,
who received the pay and
allowances of cavalry soldiers,
and could be discharged at the
discretion of the commander.

RIGHT:

**Pasig, Philippines,
Philippine–American War,
March 1899**
Oregon Volunteer Infantry
on a firing line just before
a general advance. The
Philippine–American War was
the United States' first true
colonial war as a world power.
After acquiring the Philippines
from Spain as a result of the
Spanish–American War, the
Filipino population revolted
against the new colonial ruler.

OPPOSITE:

**Colonel Theodore Roosevelt
and the Rough Riders,
Cuba, July 1898**
The victory at the Battle of
San Juan Hill led directly to
the surrender of Santiago
on July 17, a crucial victory
preceding the end of hostilities
in the Spanish–American War.

LEFT:

Fort San Antonio de Abad, Malate, Manila, 1898
An American flag flutters, hoisted to replace the Spanish colors after what has been dubbed the "Mock Battle of Manila." Local Spanish and American generals, who were legally still at war, secretly and jointly planned to transfer control of the city center from Spanish to American control, while keeping the Philippine Revolutionary Army out of the city center. The battle left American forces in control of Intramuros, the center of Manila, surrounded by Philippine forces, creating the conditions for the Battle of Manila and the start of the Philippine–American War.

OPPOSITE:

U.S. Soldiers Entrenched, Philippine–American War, 1899
The Filipinos originally fielded an irregular force of around 100,000 troops, but suffered a series of devastating losses on the battlefield against American forces equipped with superior technology and training. In 1899, the Filipinos switched from conventional to guerrilla tactics, which proved to be more effective.

OPPOSITE:

Student Army Training Corps (SATC)

In early 1918, the U.S. War Department created the Student Army Training Corps (SATC) as a way to hasten the training of soldiers during World War I. Students would enlist in the SATC and simultaneously take college courses and train for the military. Pictured here is a class in pole-climbing for telephone electricians at the University of Michigan.

ABOVE:

Bayonet Training

A sergeant instructs recruits in bayonet fighting tactics at Camp Dick, Texas, 1917. The bayonet was an important tool of close fighting prior to World War I. If all other forms of combat failed, it was also the last line of defense.

RIGHT:

Wall Scaling, Camp Wadsworth, South Carolina, 1918

Military climbing walls aim to replicate real operational conditions (from natural rock to building façades) for an optimal training environment. They are designed to cater for different types of training, including climbing, belaying, and rescue techniques, as well as engendering teamwork.

OPPOSITE:

**Infantry Charge,
World War I**

The American Expeditionary
Forces (AEF) was established
in July 1917 and numbered
more than three million by
the end of the war. Here,
American infantry attack on
the Western Front. An enemy
casualty is lying on the ground
as soldiers head toward the
smoke emanating from a
destroyed structure.

RIGHT:

**Renault FT Tanks, France,
1918**

The Renault FT was a French
light tank. When the U.S.
entered the war in April 1917
its army was short of heavy
matériel, and had no tanks at
all. France lent the American
Expeditionary Forces 144
FTs—enough to equip two
battalions.

OPPOSITE:

Mule Power, Western Front, 1918
An American private tries to move mules hauling an ammunition wagon stuck in the road at St. Baussant, east of Saint-Mihiel, France, September 1918. Despite the revolution in technology during World War I, most artillery pieces were transported by horse and cart.

LEFT:

American Soldiers Man a Hotchkiss Machine Gun, 1918
The M1914 Hotchkiss was a medium, gas operated, air-cooled, self-powered machine gun. It was the standard machine gun used by the French Army in the latter half of World War I and another example of weapons loaned to U.S. forces in theater.

ABOVE:

American Soldiers Digging a Trench, Western Front, 1917
Americans entered the trench environment with very little understanding of what awaited them. The Doughboys arrived in the front line with French arms and untried commanders, and had to adapt to the conditions of trench warfare.

LEFT:

American Soldiers Pose with a Renault FT Tank, 1918
The Renault FT was among the most revolutionary and influential tank designs in history due to it being the first production tank to have its armament within a fully rotating turret.

ABOVE:

U.S. Troops Receive Post in the Trenches, 1918
Getting letters in the post was the only reprieve from life on the Western Front and the only method of communication with loved ones at home. While British service personnel could receive letters within three days, it often took three weeks for correspondence to reach American soldiers.

OPPOSITE:

Governors Island, New York, 1931
Troops of the 16th Infantry Regiment march on Governors Island as Major General Nolan in the automobile behind them prepares to assume command of the post, December 1931. From 1821 until 1966, Governors Island was home to the United States Army and was significant for its role as a major component in the defense system of New York Harbor.

World War II

After World War I, the U.S. became a major player in international politics. The American Expeditionary Forces had proven itself a valuable military asset. When World War II came, Europe would look to the U.S. to provide support. Army Chief of Staff George C. Marshall made a gamble to send a 90-division force to Europe to fight the German threat. Due to the draft and widespread volunteerism, more than eight million soldiers filled the ranks of the Army during World War II. They landed in North Africa, Sicily, and Italy; they parachuted behind enemy lines on D-Day; they pushed enemy forces throughout France toward the German border. In the Battle of the Bulge, they fought bitterly at Bastogne, St. Vith, and in the Hürtgen Forest, to deal the final blow to German defenses.

The U.S. Army committed a quarter of its strength to the Pacific theater—about 22 divisions. While the war in Europe took precedence, the Army fought alongside the Marines in New Guinea and throughout the island-hopping campaigns and amphibious landings that characterized that theater. The Army helped to take back the island chains and famously returned to the Philippines in October 1944. In the end, it was Army General Douglas MacArthur that presided over the ceremony where Japan unconditionally surrendered to Allied forces on September 2, 1945.

OPPOSITE:
Omaha Beach, D-Day Landings, June 6, 1944
American soldiers approaching Omaha Beach in landing craft known as the Higgins boats. Omaha Beach was the second beach from the west among the five landing areas of the Normandy Invasion. It was assaulted by units of the 29th and 1st Infantry Divisions, both of which suffered high casualties in the first day's fighting.

LEFT:

Operation Torch, November 8, 1942 – May 13, 1943

U.S. and British troops offload equipment in North Africa during Operation Torch in 1942. Operation Torch intended to draw Axis forces away from the Eastern Front, thus relieving pressure on the hard-pressed Soviet Union. The operation was a compromise between U.S. and British planners, as the latter felt that the American-advocated landing in northern Europe was premature and would lead to disaster at this stage of the war.

ABOVE:

1st Ranger Battalion, Arzew, Algeria, January 1943

Rangers speed march over hilly terrain during Operation Torch. Most American troops were "green" at this stage of the war and continued training after entering the war theater. The 1st Ranger Battalion spearheaded an attack on the port of Arzew, denying the occupation of the seaport to German forces.

I WANT YOU
for the U.S. ARMY
ENLIST NOW

ABOVE:
U.S. Army Recruiting Poster
A famed World War II recruitment poster with Uncle Sam calling on young men to enlist. During the conflict, propaganda was found everywhere, almost as if to shame those who did not contribute to the war effort.

RIGHT:
93rd Infantry Division
Reactivated in May 1942, the 93rd was the first all-black division to be formed during World War II. Here, they practice an attacking formation at Fort Huachuca, AZ., 1942. The 93rd were eventually deployed to Guadalcanal in 1944, and were involved in the fighting on Morotai, Maluku, in 1945.

Invasion of Sicily, July 1943
Seated on long benches
aboard their C-47 transport,
paratroopers of the 82nd
Airborne Division smile
apprehensively en route to
Sicily and combat with the
German and Italian forces
defending the island.

**Mountain Fighting,
Italy, 1944**
Advancing up through Prato,
Italy, men of the 370th
Infantry Regiment move
toward the mountains they
will have to traverse to defeat
Germany. Attacking through
Italy, thought to be the soft
underbelly of Europe by the
British, would be a bitter fight
for U.S. troops looking for a
decisive victory.

Liberation of Rome
Rome was the first capital
to be liberated from Nazi
occupation, on June 4, 1944.
Rome had been declared an
open city, which meant that it
could be occupied without any
fighting. This was a welcome
relief after the heavily-fought
battles in the south of Italy.

OPPOSITE:

Bougainville, Solomon Islands, March 1944
Soldiers of the 129th Infantry Regiment, 37th Infantry Division, supported by a Sherman tank, battle Japanese infiltrators in the jungles of Bougainville island. The 37th Infantry Division later fought in the Philippines, entering the capital, Manila, in March 1945.

RIGHT:

165th Regimental Combat Team, Makin Atoll, Gilbert Islands, November 1943
Men of the 2nd Battalion, 165th Infantry, find it slow going in the coral-bottomed waters when assaulting Yellow Beach Two, Butaritari. The Japanese defenders chose to make their stand further inland, and it took two days of determined fighting to reduce the defenders' resistance.

Airplane Wreckage, Makin Atoll, November 1943
U.S. Army troops pause for a look at a Japanese seaplane during the battle of Makin Atoll. The plane was under repair in the lagoon when the invasion started. The Japanese used it as a defensive machine gun nest until American fliers destroyed it.

Invasion of Lingayen Gulf, Luzon, Philippines, January 1945
A line of Coast Guard landing barges, sweeping through the waters of Lingayen Gulf, carries the first wave of the Sixth Army to the beaches of Luzon, after a devastating naval bombardment of Japanese shore positions.

172nd Infantry Regiment, New Georgia, July 1943
Members of the 172nd Infantry on the Munda Trail march the five miles (eight km) to Munda Airfield, the strategic objective of the New Georgia campaign in the Allied push toward Rabaul.

LEFT:
**Normandy Campaign,
June–July 1944**
Lying in a shallow ditch along
a stone wall, American
paratroopers watch intently
for signs of enemy movement.
The soldier in the foreground
appears to be aiming his
M1 Garand rifle at a distant
target. Small unit encounters
marked the action as Allied
troops pushed inland from the
Normandy beaches.

OPPOSITE:
**Battle for Normandy,
July 11, 1944**
American howitzers shell
German forces retreating
near Carentan. The battle
of Carentan involved mainly
American airborne forces,
who first captured the town
on June 12. Carentan was
strategically important
because it sat astride the
N-13 highway as well as the
Cherbourg–Paris railroad,
which meant that in June 1944
it was also positioned between
the American landing beaches
at Utah and Omaha.

LEFT AND ABOVE:

Liberation of France

An American M8 Greyhound armored car rolls through Paris in August 1944. The Tricolor flying from the Arc de Triomphe denotes the city being liberated from Nazi rule. Initially, the Americans wanted to bypass Paris in the push towards Germany, but decided to participate in the liberation ceremony.

Of the 20,000 German troops stationed around Paris, most surrendered or fled. American GIs were seen as liberators by the French population.

In the photograph above, a U.S. soldier armed with an M1918 BAR calls for a German officer to surrender in Illy, France, September 1944.

OPPOSITE:

Normandy Campaign, August 1944

A group of American infantrymen pose in front of a wrecked enemy tank, after conducting mopping up operations in Chambois, France, the last stronghold of German forces in the Falaise Gap area.

OPPOSITE:
Airborne Invasion, Operation Market Garden, Holland, September 1944
Parachutes open overhead as waves of paratroops land in Holland during operations by the First Allied Airborne Army. The 82nd and 101st Airborne Divisions were key spearhead units, capturing bridges near Nijmegen and Eindhoven.

LEFT:
Battle of the Bulge, December 1944
A pair of GIs—one armed with an M1 Thompson submachine gun—take cover behind an abandoned German tank during the early stages of the Ardennes Offensive. The Germans launched the offensive on 16 December 1944 in an attempt to split Allied forces and capture the key port of Antwerp. By mid-January 1945 it had ground to a halt, primarily due to the efforts of the U.S. Army, which suffered more than 80,000 casualties during the campaign.

ALL PHOTOGRAPHS:
Battle of the Bulge, Belgium, January 1945
In the photograph left, American GIs of the 290th Infantry take up defensive positions amidst fresh snowfall near Amonines, Belgium. The 290th had only arrived in Europe in November 1944.

In the photograph above, American soldiers of the 289th Infantry Regiment march along the snow-covered road on their way to cut off the St. Vith–Houffalize road in Belgium. The battle at St. Vith was critical in the early stages of the defense against the German offensive.

In the photograph opposite, food is served to men of the 347th Infantry Regiment at their positions near La Roche-en-Ardennes, Belgium. As part of the newly-deployed 87th Infantry Division, the regiment was involved in repulsing and counterattacking the German offensive.

LEFT:

Crossing the Rhine River, March 26, 1945

American GIs from the 89th Division cross the Rhine under enemy fire at St. Goar, March 1945. American soldiers crouch behind the walls of the landing boat to dodge the hail of enemy bullets trying to stop their wet-gap crossing.

ABOVE:

Invasion of Germany, April 1945

Soldiers of the 55th Armored Infantry Battalion and an M4 Sherman tank of the 22nd Tank Battalion move through a smoke-filled street in Wernberg, Germany, April 22, 1945.

ABOVE:

Dash for Cover

Two anti-tank infantrymen of the 101st Infantry Regiment dash past a blazing German gasoline trailer in a square in Kronach, Germany, 1945. The 101st Infantry eventually pushed south into Czechoslovakia and Austria, where they received the surrender of many thousands of prisoners, including the whole German LXXXV Corps.

RIGHT:

Balancing Act

The barrel of a mammoth 274mm (10.78in) railroad gun captured during the U.S. Seventh Army's advance near Rentwertshausen, Germany, provides a perch for these U.S. soldiers. The railroad gun was a huge artillery piece—often surplus naval artillery—mounted on, transported by, and fired from a specially-designed railway wagon.

From the Korean Peninsula to the Balkans

The End of World War II required a shift to a new style of fighting. While the U.S. had sought a decisive victory and an unconditional surrender in World War II, the political climate of the Cold War that ensued forced soldiers to adapt to the principles of limited war. For soldiers, that change meant that tactical success did not always equal strategic victory.

The Korean War (1950–53) was the first hot war of the period. Throughout the course of the war, soldiers went through a learning period where they fought in a traditional manner while under General Douglas MacArthur and switched to limited war under General Matthew Ridgway in 1951. Korea ended in a stalemate under an armistice agreement. There was no clear definition of victory, nor would there be throughout the Cold War period. Strategically, soldiers were used as tools to fight proxy wars where the goal was to thwart the spread of communism without inciting total war and the use of nuclear weapons. The most glaring example of defeat came when the U.S. pulled out of the Vietnam conflict in 1975. While tactically successful throughout the war, the U.S. lost the strategic battle. U.S. soldiers fought limited, counterinsurgency wars through the remainder of the Cold War period in Latin America, Africa, Asia, and the Middle East in an effort to win the ideological battle that pitted western capitalism against Soviet and Chinese communism.

When the Cold War ended, U.S. soldiers spent the remaining years of the 20th century serving as part of multinational forces that attempted to restore order in war-torn Somalia, leading the strike that restored order in Haiti, and working with NATO to combat ethnic cleansing in the Balkans. The Gulf War—where a U.S.-led coalition ejected Iraqi forces from Kuwait in 1991—was the only large-scale deployment by the U.S. Army at the end of the 20th century.

OPPOSITE:
Cold War Stand-off
U.S. Army troops stand poised on Patton tanks at the Berlin Wall, October 1961. The M48 Patton was a first generation main battle tank introduced in February 1952, featuring a 90mm (3.54in) gun. It was the mainstay of the United States Army until the introduction of the M1 Abrams in the 1980s.

LEFT:

Naktong Offensive, Korea, September 1950
Men of the 9th Infantry Regiment hitch a ride on an M-26
Pershing tank to await an enemy attempt to cross the Naktong
River. The Naktong Offensive was a North Korean attack
against United Nations forces early in the Korean War, taking
place from September 1–15, 1950. It was the communist Korean
People's Army's unsuccessful final bid to break the Pusan
Perimeter established by UN forces.

ABOVE:

Machine Gun Crew, Chongchon River, Korea
Fighting with the 2nd Infantry Division north of the Chongchon
River, Sfc. Major Cleveland, weapons squad leader, points out
communist North Korean positions to his machine gun crew,
November 20, 1950. This squad are manning a belt-fed M1919
Browning .30 caliber machine gun, an illustrious weapon still
used by armed forces throughout the world today.

ABOVE:

Digging in, Korea, December 1950

These men of the Heavy Mortar Company, 7th Infantry Regiment, cook rice in their foxhole in the Kagae-dong area. As part of the United Nations forces, Army troops were forced to withdraw from the northern part of the Korean peninsula, following Chinese intervention in December 1950.

RIGHT:

Battle of Heartbreak Ridge, 1951

Infantrymen of the 27th Infantry Regiment take advantage of cover and concealment in tunnel positions, just 40 yards from communist forces. The Battle of Heartbreak Ridge was a month-long fight that took place in September–October 1951, a few miles north of the 38th parallel.

Mountain March, Korea, January 1951
Men of the 19th Infantry Regiment work their way over the snowy mountains about 10 miles (16km) north of Seoul, attempting to locate the enemy lines and positions.

OPPOSITE:

Mobile Nuclear Capability

A U.S. Army field artillery battalion load an Honest John long-range missile onto a launching vehicle during training at Grafenwoehr, Germany. The MGR-1 Honest John rocket was the first nuclear-capable, surface-to-surface rocket in the United States' arsenal. The use of nuclear weapons was designed to serve as a deterrence as the ground forces of the Soviet bloc were gaining in strength.

RIGHT:

United States Army Europe (USAREUR), West Germany, 1960

Sergeant Elvis Presley (second from left) sits with other NATO soldiers in front of a fire during the U.S. Army's Winter Shield field exercise in Bavaria. Winter Shield involved some 60,000 troops and about 15,000 vehicles. At the height of the Cold War in 1962, more than 400,000 U.S. military personnel were stationed across Europe.

LEFT:

Checkpoint Charlie, West Berlin, Germany, 1961
Army soldiers stand watch at Checkpoint Charlie. Checkpoint Charlie was the name given by the Western Allies to the best-known Berlin Wall crossing point between the two halves of the city during the Cold War.

OPPOSITE:

American Sector, West Berlin
American soldiers equipped with an M48 Patton tank stand opposite Soviet security forces at a crossing point between the American and Soviet sectors of Berlin. American troops had officially taken charge of their occupation sector in southwest Berlin on July 4, 1945. American troops remained there for almost 50 years, withdrawing finally in 1994 after the reunification of Germany.

OPPOSITE:
American Advisor, Vietnam, 1964

A U.S. Army advisor shares photos with local children. This photograph was taken during the advisory period, prior to the U.S. assuming responsibly for the fight against communist North Vietnam in 1965.

RIGHT:
Medical Evacuation, Vietnam War

Members of the 173rd Airborne Brigade load casualties into a Bell UH-1 helicopter—known as the Huey. Among the Huey's greatest strengths was its versatility. The Huey was used for troop insertion and casualty recovery. A wounded soldier could expect to be evacuated within an hour of sustaining their injuries, which had a significant effect on mortality rates.

LEFT:

**U.S. Army Armor
in Vietnam**
U.S. Army M48 tanks and
M113 ACAVs stand ready
for operations. The M113
is a fully-tracked armored
personnel carrier that was
developed and produced
to replace the mechanized
infantry's M59 APCs
from 1961.

ABOVE:

Fire Mission, Vietnam, 1965
A soldier from the 173rd
Airborne Brigade plots a fire
mission. In the background
rests an M79 grenade launcher
and a radio. The brigade was
the first major U.S. Army
ground formation deployed in
Vietnam, serving there from
1965 to 1971 and suffering
1,533 casualties.

OPPOSITE:

On Patrol, Vietnam, 1965
Soldiers of 16th Armor, 173
Airborne Brigade, move
through dense jungle in a
previously unexplored area
under Viet Cong control near
Ben Cat, north of Saigon,
September 1965. These
men are armed with what
was then the new M16A1
automatic rifle.

Air Supply

C-7 Caribou transport planes offload men and matériel in Vietnam. The C-7 was a Canadian-made tactical airlifter designed for the U.S. Army to supply the battlefront with troops and supplies and evacuate casualties on the return journey.

RIGHT:

"Search and Destroy" Mission, April 1967

Soldiers from the 1st Cavalry Division touch down into a landing zone in rural Vietnam. The Bell UH-1B Huey was the workhorse for air cavalry operations during the Vietnam War. "Search and Destroy" (S&D) became the cornerstone of U.S. military strategy in Vietnam. Ground forces would be inserted into hostile territory, search out the enemy, bring them to battle, and withdraw immediately afterward.

LEFT:

9th Infantry Division, Tet Offensive, 1968
A soldier from the 9th Infantry Division aims his M16A1 assault rifle while on patrol during the Tet Offensive. The division operated in the Mekong Delta from 1967 to 1972. U.S. commander in Vietnam General Westmoreland stated that the actions of the 9th Infantry were one of the main reason the Viet Cong did not overrun the Delta region at this time.

OPPOSITE:

Clearing Operation, Nui Ba Den, Vietnam, August 1970
Men from B Company, 1st Battalion, 27th Infantry Regiment (the "Wolfhounds"), 25th Infantry Division, cross a stream during a search and clear operation near Fire Support Base Kien, 10 miles (16km) southeast of Nui Ba Den.

OPPOSITE:

NBC Warfare

Army soldiers wear NBC (nuclear, biological, chemical) gear in May 1987. Pictured here in their chemical suits, they train to remain capable of responding to the threats of modern warfare.

ABOVE:

Invasion of Panama, December 1989

Army soldiers exit a helicopter and head towards cover in Santiago on December 23, 1989, during the invasion of Panama to oust General Manuel Antonio Noriega.

ABOVE:

M198 Howitzer, Operation Desert Storm, 1990–91
U.S. forces prepare to fire during a live firing exercise while training in Saudi Arabia before the allied intervention in Kuwait, December 1990. The U.S. Army was deployed in the Persian Gulf following Iraq's invasion of Kuwait on August 2, 1990.

RIGHT:

Armored Column, Operation Desert Storm, 1990–91
U.S. Army armored fighting vehicles (AFVs) from the 24th Infantry Division are unloaded during military maneuvers in Saudi Arabia. The 24th Infantry Division had the key role of first blocking the Euphrates River valley to cut off Iraqi forces in Kuwait, and then attacking east in coordination with VII Corps to defeat the armor-heavy divisions of the Iraqi Republican Guard. During the short campaign, the division's forces were expanded to 25,000 troops and more than 400 M1 Abrams and M2 Bradley AFVs.

OPPOSITE:

Airborne Deployment, Operation Desert Shield, 1990

American troops at Dahran airport in Saudi Arabia, August 23, 1990. Dahran is where the first units of the XVIII Airborne Corps began deploying once the decision to fight Iraqi incursion into Kuwait was made.

ABOVE:

Kosovo Crisis, 1999

U.S. soldiers at a camp near Tirana, Albania, man an M249 light machine gun during the Kosovo crisis. As part of NATO forces, American units were deployed in Kosovo to force the Serbian Milosevic regime to withdraw armed militias and facilitate the return of refugees.

RIGHT:

Bosnian War, 1995

Sergeant Steve Norris and Lieutenant Jeff Schall stand watch next to their M2 Bradley IFV as work on a pontoon bridge over the Sava River continues. U.S. troops were deployed to the Balkans as part of SFOR— Stabilisation Force in Bosnia and Herzegovina.

LEFT:

Army Peacekeepers, Tuzla, Bosnia

U.S. Army troops work with Bosnian Serbs on creating boundaries for the Zone of Separation north of Tuzla. Tuzla was the headquarters of the 1st Armored Division (1AD) Task Force, designated as "Task Force Eagle" (TFE). Comprised of over 19,000 soldiers, TFE was the U.S. component of a force of 60,000 troops deployed by NATO to separate the warring factions in Bosnia.

RIGHT:

Overwatch Duties, Kosovo, 2004

A U.S. soldier watches over a checkpoint between the Pristina and Nitrovica highway. In 2004, NATO dispatched hundreds of extra soldiers to Kosovo to clamp down on violence which had left 22 dead in the worst violence since the 1999 war in the UN-run Serbian province.

Training

Army soldiers train throughout their careers. They are required to pass the Army Combat Fitness Test (ACFT) twice a year to remain on active duty. The test is designed to ensure that all soldiers can reasonably endure the rigors of combat—carrying their gear on long marches or fighting in unfavorable terrain. The ACFT, however, is basic-level training for Army soldiers. They must commit to a disciplined training regimen to ensure success on the test and in their units.

Soldiers train daily in their respective branches at installations around the world to hone their skills and function efficiently. The multi-domain fights they train for make it necessary to not only master different terrain—mountain, jungle, desert, etc.—but also ever-evolving technology. While Special Operations soldiers train in special weapons, languages, and regional skills, doctors have to continually train to better practice battlefield medicine, while pilots have to hone their skills in troop insertion, supporting ground operations, and troop extraction. Soldiers in the armored branch have to become masters of their vehicles and soldiers in artillery units have to constantly practice to maintain efficiency. All combat specialties have to be able to fight as a coordinated effort. Soldiers are constantly assessed to ensure that they are, indeed, masters in their assigned field.

OPPOSITE:
Basic Military Mountaineering Course
Soldiers climb Smugglers' Notch during the final phase of the Basic Military Mountaineering Course in Jeffersonville, Vermont. Students in the Basic Military Mountaineering course spend two weeks acquiring the skills and knowledge required to operate in mountainous terrain.

ABOVE AND RIGHT:

U.S. Army Special Forces Command Mountaineering Program

Soldiers participate in Senior Course Level II training near Fort Carson, Colorado. Team members learn 15 basic tasks, including navigating in mountainous terrain, rope commands, transportation of a casualty on an improvised litter, and advanced rappelling techniques. During Level II, the soldiers are expected to know and pass a hands-on test on the basic fundamentals of rock climbing. Throughout the training soldiers recover weapons caches from the top of mountains and abandoned mine shafts using a variety of rope techniques.

**101st Airborne Conduct
Rappel Training**
Frequent training insures
success in operations, whether
involved in air assaults—
where soldiers rappel from
helicopters—or rappelling
down the side of a sheer
training wall.

LEFT AND ABOVE:

Army Combat Fitness Test (ACFT)

Pictured left, a soldier keeps in shape by lifting weights. Here, she performs the deadlift, an exercise every soldier is required to demonstrate for their Army-mandated fitness evaluation.

Pictured above, a soldier from the New Jersey Army National Guard carries two 40-pound (18kg) kettlebells.

The soldiers are being trained for their Level II certification, which will enable them to serve as the noncommissioned officer in charge of the test and grade soldiers being tested. The ACFT consists of six events: strength deadlift; standing power throw; hand-release pushup; sprint, drag, carry; leg tuck; and a two-mile (3.2km) run.

Squat Lift
Army Staff Sergeant Angel
Ortiz with the 25th Infantry
Division squats during a
weight lifting competition
in Cash Gym in Forward
Operating Base Warhorse,
Diyala province, Iraq.

Ten-Mile Race
Soldiers take part in the
Army Ten Miler at Forward
Operating Base Shindand,
Afghanistan. The event was
hosted by the 1st Air Cavalry
Brigade, 1st Cavalry Division,
Task Force Spearhead.
The annual race is used to
promote the Army, build
esprit de corps, support Army
fitness goals, and enhance
community relations.

**Ranger Training,
Fort Benning, Georgia**
The David E. Grange Jr.
Best Ranger Competition is
an annual event hosted by
the Airborne and Ranger
Training Brigade. It is a
two-man team tournament
where competitors must be
active service military and
Ranger qualified.

OPPOSITE:

Oregon Best Warrior Competition

An Oregon Army National Guard soldier from the 82nd Cavalry Regiment high-crawls through the surf in full battle gear for the Omaha Beach event during the 2017 Oregon Best Warrior Competition at Camp Rilea, Oregon. Once on shore, the competitors carry two cement-filled ammunition canisters to the top of a steep sand dune and then race back down to the finish line.

RIGHT:

Stress Shooting with an M4 Carbine

A soldier from the 1st Battalion (Assault), 150th Aviation Regiment, is assessed during the stress shoot portion of the New Jersey Army National Guard's Best Warrior Competition. During this part of the competition, the soldiers are evaluated on high and low crawl, sled drag, medical evaluation, nine-line medical evacuation request, M249 machine gun breakdown, and an M9 pistol and M4 carbine tactical shoot.

LEFT:

Confidence Course Training
Soldiers of A Company, 412th Aviation Support Battalion, 12th Combat Aviation Brigade, navigate confidence course training as part of their pre-deployment training. The event is also designed to foster camaraderie, boost morale, and build esprit de corps among soldiers before active deployments, in this case to Afghanistan.

OPPOSITE:

Obstacle Course
U.S. Army Spc. Michael Meng assigned to 3rd Squadron, 2nd Cavalry Regiment, overcomes an obstacle during the regiment's noncommissioned officer and soldier of the quarter competition at the Seventh Army Training Command's Grafenwoehr Training Area, Germany, 2018.

OPPOSITE:
Ranger Training
A soldier climbs the net as part of the Best Ranger Competition. The average participant is 28 years of age, around 5'10" (1.77m) tall, and is in peak physical condition.

RIGHT:
IMT Training, Camp Ravenna Joint Maneuver Training Center, Ohio
Crawling through mud, a soldier from the 37th Infantry Brigade Combat Team, Ohio National Guard, searches for the next covered fighting position during individual movement techniques (IMT) training. The IMT is just one of more than 200 typical training tasks that soldiers must complete before they go on active deployment.

OPPOSITE:

Mass Jump, Fort Bragg, North Carolina
Soldiers from the 82nd Airborne Division perform a mass jump with 120 members. The 82nd Airborne Division's real-world mission is to strategically deploy, conduct forcible entry parachute assault, and secure key objectives for follow-on military operations, within 18 hours of notification.

ABOVE:

High Altitude Low Opening (HALO) Training
A member of a Special Forces Operations (SFO) detachment jumps from a UH-60 Black Hawk helicopter during High Altitude Low Opening (HALO) training. Northern Edge is Alaska's annual joint training exercise designed to enhance interoperability among the services by honing joint service procedures.

RIGHT:

Parachute Training
A paratrooper from Special Operations Detachment (NATO) drags his parachute during Leapfest 2016 in West Kingston, R.I. Leapfest is an international parachute training event and competition hosted by the 56th Troop Command, Rhode Island Army National Guard, to promote high level technical training for airborne soldiers.

LEFT:

Spotting Scope, Sniper Training

An Army Paratrooper assigned to 1st Battalion, 503rd Infantry Regiment, uses his spotting scope during sniper training as part of Exercise Eagle Sokol at Pocek Range in Slovenia. A spotting scope allows recognition and identification of targets at long distances.

OPPOSITE:

Live-Fire Exercises

Soldiers assigned to the 18th Combat Sustainment Support Battalion set up an M18A1 claymore anti-personnel mine during live-fire training at the Grafenwoehr Training Area in Germany.

OPPOSITE:
Sniper Training
A paratrooper assigned to 503rd Infantry Regiment, 173rd Airborne Brigade, engages targets with a M2010 Enhanced Sniper Rifle during sniper training.

LEFT:
Fire Exercise
Corporal William Lamm, a non-commissioned officer with 1st Cavalry Regiment, 2nd Stryker Brigade Combat Team, 2nd Infantry Division, directs soldiers during an incipient fire exercise on Camp Nathan Smith, Afghanistan. Soldiers who complete the course act as first responders if fires occur.

LEFT TOP:
Simulated Convoy Training
A sergeant in the Army National Guard talks to her team as driver Pfc. Lucas Graham (right) maneuvers through simulated convoy training. The simulator allows the soldiers to talk back and forth while watching their progress on computer screens embedded in their goggles.

ABOVE:
Grenade Throwing
A soldier lies down behind a covered position and lobs a grenade at his target as part of grenade training exercises.

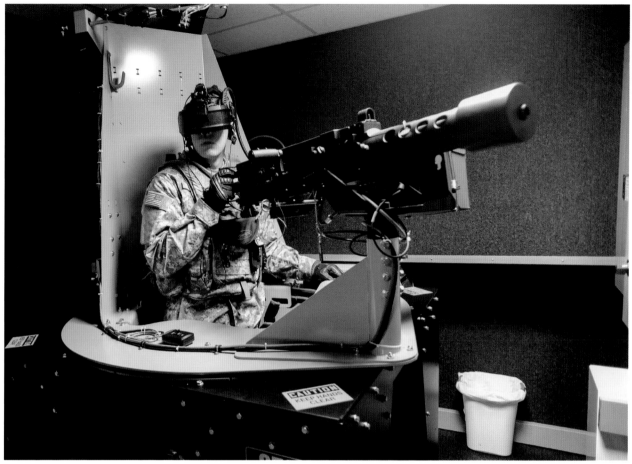

LEFT:

Beretta M9 Handgun Practice

Soldiers attached to Bravo Company, 445th Civil Affairs Battalion, participate in tactical range training using M9 semi-automatic pistols at Normandy Range Complex, Basra, Iraq. All soldiers are required to qualify with their assigned weapon every 12 months.

ABOVE:

Virtual Clearance Training Suite (VCTS)

Pfc. Cullen Rocha sits on the gunner station while training in the Virtual Clearance Training Suite (VCTS) at Grafenwoehr, Germany. The VCTS allows soldiers to learn and master all tasks likely to be encountered during clearance missions, without risk to man or machine.

OPPOSITE:

Improvised Explosive Device (IED) Training

A sergeant with Engineer Troop, 4th Squadron, 2nd Cavalry Regiment, controls a Talon explosive ordnance disposal robot from inside an armored vehicle, using it to destroy an improvised explosive device during pre-deployment training. The Army use Husky Metal Detecting and Marking Vehicles, RG-31 Mk3A armored fighting vehicles, and Buffalo Mine-Protected Clearance Vehicles to conduct counter-IED operations.

RIGHT:

Combat Water Survival Training, Fort Hunter Liggett, California

A combat engineer from the 374th Engineer Company (Sapper), swims 82ft (25m) with a rucksack and a dummy weapon. Combat Water Survival Training is a two-week field exercise known as a Sapper Leader Course Prerequisite Training. The unit grades soldiers on various events to determine which ones will earn a spot on a "merit list" to attend the Sapper Leader Course at Fort Leonard Wood, Missouri.

OPPOSITE:
Search-and-Rescue Exercise
Army Sergeant
Nathan McLaughlin, a
standardization instructor,
rescues Staff Sergeant
Christian Larsen, who plays
the part of a lost hiker
during a search-and-rescue
training exercise, at Camp
W.G. Williams, Riverton,
Utah. Pictured here, the two
are being lifted to the rescue
helicopter hovering above.

RIGHT:
Air Assault School
Students wait for a signal to
rappel from a UH-60 Black
Hawk helicopter during Air
Assault School at Fort Bliss,
Texas. Once finished with
the school, these soldiers will
continuously hone the skills
they learned in their home
units to ensure success in
future missions.

ABOVE:
Boat Drills
Corporal Denise Houston hangs on to a Zodiac boat as she, along with fellow soldiers, try to get the watercraft turned back over at Fort Leonard Wood's Training Area 250 Lake. Her unit was tasked with completing many tests, including boat drills and swimming with waterproofed gear.

RIGHT:
Small Boat Movement Training
Army Rangers undertake small boat movement training. Small boats are a common insertion and extraction tool to get Rangers—and other special forces—into, and out of, the fight.

LEFT:

Combined Operations, 160th Special Operations Aviation Regiment

Special Warfare Combatant-craft Crewmen from the Navy's Special Boat Team 12 conduct a Maritime External Air Transportation System (MEATS) training evolution in Moses Lake, Washington, with the help of an Army MH-47G Chinook helicopter. MEATS is a way to quickly move a watercraft from a point on land or water to somewhere else. The crewmen rig the boat to the helicopter as it hovers above, and then climb a rope ladder to board the helicopter, before moving to the final destination, where they will slide down a rope to the boat before the helicopter disconnects the hoist cables.

ABOVE:

DUNKER Training

An aviator with 2nd Battalion, 25th Aviation Regiment, swims to the surface during DUNKER training. The training teaches aviators and crewmembers the water survival skills necessary to evacuate a helicopter if it becomes immersed underwater.

Water Insertions
Mississippi Army National Guard soldiers with 2nd Battalion, 20th Special Forces Group (Airborne), practice water insertions. This type of training increases readiness for state emergencies and missions overseas.

Dismounted Zone Reconnaissance

Cavalry scouts for the 82nd Cavalry Regiment navigate rough terrain on foot while conducting dismounted zone reconnaissance training at the Yakima Training Center, Washington. The training is part of a large-scale exercise known as eXportable Combat Training Capability (XCTC), which focuses on improving individual and team skillsets, decision making, equipment familiarization, and deployment readiness.

Robot Control Station

Soldiers from the 95th Chemical Company set up a CUGR Chemical, Biological, Radiological, and Nuclear Unmanned Ground Reconnaissance robot control station in Alaska.

LEFT:

Counter-reconnaissance Exercise

Army Sergeant Jimmie Wu of Able Company, 2nd Battalion, 503rd Infantry Regiment, 173rd Airborne Brigade, employs a satellite antenna during a counter-reconnaissance scenario during exercise Saber Junction 16 at the U.S. Army's Joint Multinational Readiness Center (JMRC) in Hohenfels, Germany. The exercise was designed to evaluate the readiness of the Army's Europe-based combat brigades to conduct unified land operations and promote interoperability in a multinational environment. Saber Junction 16 included nearly 5,000 soldiers from 16 NATO and European partner nations.

OPPOSITE:

Surveillance Training

Soldiers man and secure a surveillance site in phase two of Reconnaissance Surveillance Leaders Course at Fort Benning, Georgia. Students train to observe NIAs (named areas of interest) and establish communication with higher headquarters.

BELOW:

Making a Shelter

Soldiers of 1st Squadron, 91st Cavalry Regiment, 173rd Airborne Brigade, construct a tent while conducting tactical operations during exercise Saber Junction 16.

RIGHT:

Reconnaissance Exercise

Armed with an M249 squad automatic weapon (SAW), soldiers of 503rd Infantry Regiment, 173rd Airborne Brigade, scan their sector of fire during a counter-reconnaissance offensive during exercise Saber Junction 16.

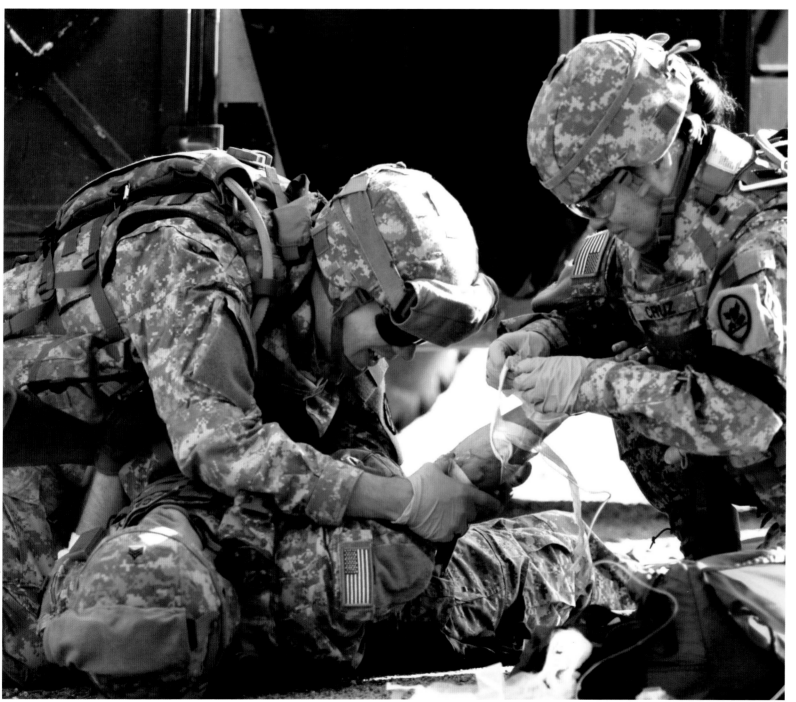

Combat Support Hospital

Captain Michelle Chador, center, a registered nurse with the 345th Combat Support Hospital, holds an intravenous (IV) bag as a wounded soldier is evaluated by the medical team in the Emergency Medical Treatment area of a field hospital.

LEFT:

Simulated Casualty

Army officers Andrew Richardson and Kim Cruz, both of the 131st Mobile Public Affairs Detachment, remove a needle and taping gauze from a simulated casualty during medical training at Fort Dix, N.J. The soldiers are being trained by First Army Public Affairs in preparation for a mission in support of U.S. Army Central Command (CENTCOM). CENTCOM deploys troops to the Middle East, Central Asia, and parts of South Asia.

Aeromedical Evacuation
Soldiers assigned to the 2-211th General Support Aviation Battalion, Minnesota Army National Guard, and the 155th Armored Brigade Combat Team, Mississippi Army National Guard, pull a patient from a UH-60L Black Hawk helicopter during an aeromedical evacuation rehearsal at Camp Buehring, Kuwait. The rehearsal was conducted to prepare for Operation Desert Observer II, a combined arms live-fire exercise with Task Force Spartan and the Kuwaiti Land Forces.

Weapons and Vehicles

A rmy soldiers have the world's greatest technology at their disposal. The development of new weapons, vehicles, and technology is of paramount importance if the Army is to continue being able to fight successfully in future engagements. The Humvee, Army Ground Mobility Vehicle (A-GMV), Light Combat Tactical All-Terrain Vehicle (L-ATV), multiple tanks, and various assault and troop-carrying helicopters and planes, ensure that U.S. soldiers can both get to the fight and operate effectively in a multi-domain environment. Nothing is quite as menacing as facing down the gun barrel of an M1 Abrams tank, or watching the destruction wrought by an Apache assault helicopter. All of the vehicles employed by Army soldiers have some mounted weapons system. Soldiers also carry personal weapons like pistols, assault rifles, sniper rifles, shotguns, grenade launchers, and explosives. The constant upgrading of multiple variations of all these weapons ensure the modern Army soldier has the correct tools to be effective.

The Army also deploys larger munitions, like the M777A2 155mm (6.1in) medium towed howitzer, the M109A7 Paladin 155mm self-propelled howitzer, and the M142 High Mobility Rocket Artillery System (HIMARS), to name a few. Nuclear weapons remain the deadliest form of weaponry and the most assured to promote deterrence, especially with the advent of tactical warheads and missile systems that make accuracy easier to achieve.

OPPOSITE:
Mine Resistant Ambush Protected (MRAP)
A paratrooper with the 82nd Airborne Division's 1st Brigade Combat Team aims his M4 carbine at insurgents in Ghazni province, Afghanistan. The vehicle he is using for cover is a Mine Resistant Ambush Protected (MRAP) vehicle. MRAPs are designed specifically to withstand improvised explosive device (IED) detonations.

OPPOSITE:

M1 Abrams Tank
Gunnery Qualifications
Soldiers from the 116th
Cavalry Regiment, Idaho
Army National Guard,
complete live-fire gunnery
qualifications at the Orchard
Combat Training Center,
Idaho. The M1 Abrams is the
U.S. Army's main battle tank
and has been in service since
the 1980s, having proved its
capabilities in the Persian
Gulf War, Afghanistan,
and Iraq.

RIGHT:

M1 Abrams Tank
Live-Fire Exercise
An M1 Abrams tank from
2nd Armored Brigade
Combat Team, 1st Infantry
Division, fires a round during
a Combined Arms Live Fire
Exercise (CALFEX). The
CALFEX integrates all forms
of firepower an armored
brigade combat team (ABCT)
and their enablers bring to a
fight, while making sure the
company masses their effects
on an enemy at the right time
and place.

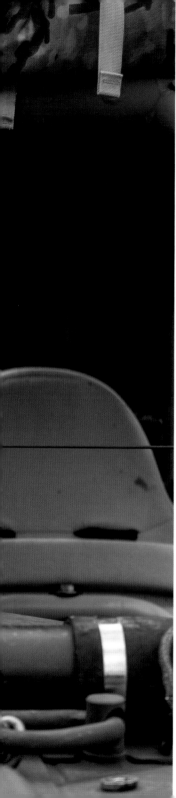

LEFT:

Army Ground Mobility Vehicle (A-GMV)

A soldier from 503rd Parachute Infantry Regiment (PIR) drives an Army Ground Mobility Vehicle (A-GMV) for the first time, during an air assault rehearsal at Udbina Airbase, Croatia. The A-GMV is an airdroppable light off-road vehicle designed to improve the mobility of light infantry brigades. It can be carried externally by a UH-60 Black Hawk helicopter.

ABOVE:

M2 Bradley Infantry Fighting Vehicle

Pfc. Joseph Salerna backs an M2 Bradley Infantry Fighting Vehicle (IFV) aboard a C-17 Globemaster III aircraft with the help of an Air Force loadmaster at Lawson Army Airfield, Fort Benning, Georgia. Salerna was part of an element from 2-69 Armor participating in a large-scale training exercise designed to prepare units for rapid deployments across the globe.

M113 Armored Personnel Carrier

Soldiers assigned to the 4th Infantry Regiment engage a target from an M113A2 APC during squad maneuver training. First introduced in the 1960s, the M113 has developed through various iterations, including armored ambulance, mortar carrier, engineer vehicle, and command vehicle. Today, the type is rarely used for frontline service, having been replaced by the M2 and M3 Bradley IFVs.

OPPOSITE:

High Mobility Multipurpose Wheeled Vehicle (Humvee)

Soldiers from the 2nd Cavalry Regiment maneuver a Humvee through a driver's training terrain course as part of a basic driving class at the Seventh Army Training Command's Grafenwoehr Training Area, Germany. The new driver's training complex is comprised of a series of 11 man-made and natural obstacles spread across a 4.7-mile (7.6km) area. Each of the obstacles is specifically designed to challenge and train soldiers in a variety of U.S. and multinational military vehicles and AFVs.

LEFT:

Common Remotely Operated Weapon Station (CROWS)

Spc. Warren Feeley from 25th Infantry Division looks through a fire control system inside an M1126 Infantry Carrier Vehicle (ICV) while engaging targets with a .50-caliber Remote Weapons System, during a live-fire training exercise at Pohakuloa Training Area (PTA), Hawaii.

OPPOSITE:

M1150 Assault Breacher Vehicle (ABV)

Soldiers from 116th Brigade Engineer Battalion position their M1150 Assault Breacher Vehicle during a live-fire training exercise at the National Training Center (NTC) in Fort Irwin, California. The M1150 is a mine and explosives clearing vehicle, equipped with a mine-plough and line charges. NTC is a month-long rotation that provides more than 4,000 service members with realistic training to enhance their combat, support, and sustainment capabilities.

Stryker Infantry Carrier Vehicle (ICV)
Soldiers from 1st Cavalry Regiment, 2nd Brigade, 1st Armored Division, dismount from a Stryker vehicle during a training exercise at Dona Ana Range, New Mexico. The eight-wheeled Stryker has a good reputation for its mobility and for offering effective protection to soldiers on deployment in Iraq and Afghanistan.

OPPOSITE:
Stryker Gunnery Training
Cavalry troopers from 14th Cavalry Regiment, 2nd Stryker Brigade Combat Team, 25th Infantry Division, maneuver a Stryker-mounted M2 .50-caliber machine gun via the Remote Weapon System as part of Stryker gunnery training at Yakima Training Center, Washington.

OPPOSITE:

MRZR 2 Ultralight All-Terrain Vehicle

A paratrooper from the 82nd Airborne Division drives the Brigade's new Light Tactical All Terrain Vehicle (LTATV) during training at Fort Bragg, N.C. In 2014, the 1st Battalion, 325th AIR, were the first unit to exercise and assess the added capabilities of the new LTATVs. These ultralight vehicles are designed for expeditionary forces and provide foot soldiers with the ability to move much faster. They can be airlifted internally by CH-47 Chinook or CH-53 helicopters.

ABOVE:

High Mobility Artillery Rocket System (HIMARS)

Crews from the 133rd Field Artillery Regiment, attached to the 71st Expeditionary Military Intelligence Brigade, 36th Infantry Division, Texas Army National Guard, fire High Mobility Artillery Rocket System (HIMARS) during a demonstration at Fort Hood, Texas. First developed in the 1990s, the light multiple rocket launcher is intended to destroy enemy artillery, trucks, light armor, personnel carriers, troop concentrations, and supplies.

OPPOSITE:

Soltam K6 Mortar

Spc. Gareth Warner drops a 120mm (4.75in) mortar round into the barrel during a fire mission at Combat Outpost Zurok in Paktika province, Afghanistan. Made in Israel, the Soltam K6 is the long-range version of the Soltam K5 and has replaced older systems, such as the 107mm (4.2in) M30, in the U.S. Army.

ABOVE:

Fire Practice

Rangers assigned to 2nd Battalion, 75th Ranger Regiment, fire a 120mm (4.75in) mortar during a tactical training exercise on Camp Roberts, California. Rangers constantly train to maintain the highest level of tactical proficiency.

RIGHT:

Rapid Infiltration Exercise

High Mobility Artillery Rocket Systems return to their C-17 Globemaster III aircraft after a HIMARS Rapid Infiltration (HI-RAIN) demonstration. The exercise includes rocket artillery being flown to a firing point by C-17, deploying from the aircraft, firing at a target, then rapidly extracting. The training operation can be completed in under five hours.

CAUTION

CONNECTOR IN TAS MOUNT
MUST BE LOWERED
BEFORE MOUNTING OR
DISMOUNTING TAS

OPPOSITE:

BGM-71 TOW Missile System

A soldier from the 3rd Battalion, 172nd Infantry Regiment, peers through the viewfinder of a TOW anti-tank guided missile system during a training exercise at Camp Ethan Allen Training Site. The BGM-71 TOW is an American anti-tank missile that can be fitted on a tripod-mounted launch tube and various military vehicles to launch missiles from a stationary position.

RIGHT:

FGM-148 Javelin

Infantry fire an FGM-148 Javelin during a combined arms live-fire exercise in support of Eager Lion. Eager Lion is an annual, two-week multilateral exercise hosted by the Hashemite Kingdom of Jordan, designed to exchange military expertise and improve interoperability among partner nations.

M119 Howitzer
Soldiers assigned to 77th Field Artillery Regiment, 4th Brigade Combat Team, 4th Infantry Division, fire a 105mm (4.13in) round from an M119 howitzer during live-fire training at Combat Outpost Monti, Kunar province, Afghanistan. The howitzer provides direct and indirect fire support to the forces deployed in combined arms operations.

RIGHT:
Refurbished D-30 Howitzer
Sergeant First Class Fredrick Edwards fires a 122mm (4.8in) D-30 howitzer at Kabul Military Training Center, Afghanistan. Dating from the Cold War era and produced in vast numbers, the Soviet-made D-30 is still in service in more than 60 countries. These test fires are the final step for this refurbished artillery weapon.

Talon Tracked Military Robot

Pictured opposite, a combat engineer with the 122nd Engineer Clearance Company, South Carolina National Guard, conducts route clearance training using the Talon IV Reset robotic vehicle in preparation for a deployment. Soldiers practiced finding, targeting, and disposing of improvised explosive devices (IEDs) and ordnance to keep routes clear and safe in a combat environment.

Pictured right, an NCO with the 323rd Engineering Clearance Company operates a Talon tracked military robot by using a ground remote on a route clearance mission while on a Combat Support Training Exercise. The Talon carries sensors and a robotic manipulator. It has been deployed by the U.S. Army since 2000, primarily for detecting, disarming, or destroying improvised explosive devices (IED) in the conflicts in Iraq and Afghanistan.

LEFT AND ABOVE:

M240B Machine Gun

Pictured left, brass ammunition casings litter the ground as a soldier qualifies with the M240B machine gun.

Pictured above, looking through the sight of his 240B, a paratrooper pulls security during a training exercise.

RIGHT TOP:

M249 Squad Automatic Weapon (SAW)

Tracer rounds spit from an M249 machine gun. Tracers are a special type of bullet with a small pyrotechnic charge at the base. When fired, the powder material ignites and burns brightly. The bullet leaves a trail you can see without the aid of optics.

RIGHT:

M2 Browning .50 Cal Heavy Machine Gun

Fire practice at Novo Selo Training Range, Bulgaria. The M2 has an illustrious history with U.S. armed forces—developed in the 1930s, it has featured in every major conflict since.

OPPOSITE:
M-4 Carbine

An officer from the 1-182nd Infantry Regiment of the Rhode Island National Guard fires his M-4 rifle during a training mission near Forward Operating Base Mehtar Lam in Laghman province, Afghanistan. Weapons training while on deployment is crucial if soldiers are to maintain operational effectiveness.

RIGHT:
Hydra 70 Rockets, AH-64 Apache Helicopter

A soldier from 4th Battalion, 227th Attack Reconnaissance Battalion, 1st Cavalry, loads an AH-64 Apache with 70mm/2.75in rockets during a Forward Arming and Refueling Point exercise near Camp Buehring, Kuwait. The Hydra 70 is a fin-stabilized unguided rocket used primarily in the air-to-ground role.

ABOVE:
M320 Grenade Launcher Firing Practice
Staff Sergeant Jonathan Anderson, 2017 Army Reserve Best
Warrior NCO Runner-up, shoots an M320 grenade launcher
as part of preparation for an upcoming competition.

RIGHT:
AT4 Anti-tank Weapon
A paratrooper with 2nd Battalion, 503rd Infantry Regiment,
173rd Airborne Brigade, carries an AT4 training grenade
launcher during a platoon-level live-fire exercise. The AT4 is
an 84mm (3.3in) unguided, portable, single-shot, recoilless
smoothbore anti-tank weapon built in Sweden. The AT4 has
been in service with the Army since the late 1980s.

RQ-7 Shadow Unmanned Aerial Vehicle

Spc. Mark Daves, an unmanned aerial vehicle maintainer with 3rd Stryker Brigade Combat Team, 2nd Infantry Division, pushes a Shadow UAV down the runway. Since its introduction in the early 2000s, the RQ-7 has mainly been employed for reconnaissance missions.

RQ-11 Raven B Unmanned Aerial Vehicle

A corporal from the 258th Field Artillery, New York Army National Guard, performs a systems check on an RQ-11 Raven B, a small unmanned aerial system, during the field training portion of the 1st Battalion, 254th Regional Training Institute (Combat Arms), unmanned aerial system Raven operator's course.

CH-47 Chinook Helicopter

Soldiers from 173rd Airborne Brigade Combat Team dismount from a CH-47 Chinook helicopter during training at the Joint Multinational Training Center in Hohenfels, Germany, in preparation for their upcoming deployment to Afghanistan. Soldiers refine their skills in mounted and dismounted patrols, small unit tactics, operations in urban terrain, and counter-improvised explosive devices.

Mobile Artillery

A UH-60 Black Hawk helicopter, piloted by members of the 4th Combat Aviation Brigade, 4th Infantry Division, picks up an M119 howitzer during air assault training, testing the Army's capabilities to get necessary material to the fight.

Operations in the 21st Century

The U.S. Army has been constantly engaged in war since the turn of the century. On September 11, 2001, the Al-Qaeda terrorist group led by Osama bin Laden coordinated an attack against the United States. The Army, as part of U.S. and UN coalition forces, deployed to Afghanistan to hunt down and destroy the Al-Qaeda network. On May 1, 2012, President Obama and President Karzai signed the Enduring Strategic Partnership Agreement between the Islamic Republic of Afghanistan and the United States of America. The Agreement provides for the possibility of U.S. forces in Afghanistan after 2014, for the purposes of training Afghan forces and targeting the remnants of Al-Qaeda.

From 2003–2010, U.S. Army soldiers were deployed to Iraq, following the successful invasion and removal of the dictator Saddam Hussein. The U.S. is still committed to providing support to Iraq for further development in the areas of defense and security; education and culture; energy; human rights; services; and trade—all of which has required the Army to maintain a small force in the country. In 2011, soldiers were deployed to Libya as part of a NATO force that assisted rebel forces against the government of Muammar Gaddafi. In 2012, tensions rose once again in Iraq and neighboring Syria, where a new group—the Islamic State of Iraq and the Levant (ISIL)—declared an Islamic caliphate and rapidly seized territory. They began a widespread propaganda campaign to cultivate domestic terrorism in other countries and to recruit new members. The Army deployed with its sister services and other NATO allies to contain and reverse the spread of ISIL. From 2012–2018 the war raged, until ISIL no longer held any territory in Iraq and had severely declined in Syria.

Today, the Army deploys troops in many countries around the world, with large numbers stationed in Germany and South Korea in support of America's allies.

OPPOSITE:
On Patrol
Soldiers engage Taliban forces during a halt to repair a disabled vehicle near the village of Allah Say, Afghanistan. They are pictured here crouching behind their Humvees for cover.

LEFT:

AH-64 Apache Attack Helicopter

An Army Apache attack helicopter prepares to depart Bagram Air Field, Afghanistan, January 2012. Equipped with a powerful array of weapons, including rockets, missiles, and the M230 Chain Gun—the Apache conducts insertions, precision strikes against targets, and provides armed reconnaissance in support of ground troops.

OPPOSITE:

Search Mission

CH-47 Chinook helicopters prepare to land on a pick-up zone to transport soldiers who were on a weapons cache search mission in Landikheyl, a mountainous region of Afghanistan.

LEFT AND ABOVE:

Building Relationships

Pictured left, a child from Angla Kala village gives a high five to Spc. Jesus B. Fernandez. International Security Assistance Force troops regularly meet with village elders to improve communications between residents and government officials.

Pictured above, members of the Kandahar Provincial Reconstruction Team (PRT) hand out pens to local Afghan children during a site assessment of the Dowry Rud Check Dam, Kandaha province. The PRT works with government officials at the district and provincial levels to build sustainable infrastructure capacity.

LEFT:

Battalion Commander
Lieutenant Colonel Kimo Gallahue of 2nd Battalion, 87th Infantry Regiment, 3rd Brigade Combat Team, 10th Mountain Division, surveys the site where an improvised explosive device (IED) killed two of his men, in Nerkh district, Wardak province, Afghanistan.

ABOVE:

Carpentry Specialist
An Army carpentry and masonry specialist with the 585th Engineer Company hammers a nail into a B-hut being built for Task Force Spartan. Units in Task Force Spartan provide capabilities such as aviation, logistics, force protection, and information management.

OPPOSITE:

Building a Checkpoint
Soldiers from the 5th Stryker Brigade Combat Team, 2nd Infantry Division, construct an Afghan Highway Police checkpoint in Robat, Afghanistan, to improve intelligence sharing among Afghan security forces.

LEFT:

Designated Marksman
A designated marksman watches the surrounding ridge lines for enemy activity in Kajaki, Paktika province, Afghanistan. Using his scope to scan the terrain, this soldier is armed with an M110 Semi Automatic Sniper System (SASS), now widely used as a squad marksman weapon.

OPPOSITE:

Overwatch Duties
Scouts from 2nd Battalion, 503rd Infantry Regiment (Airborne), carry out overwatch from a mountain face during Operation Destined Strike, while 2nd Platoon, Able Company, searches a village below the Chowkay Valley in Kunar province, Afghanistan.

OPPOSITE:

Cave Search

With their 5.56mm M4 carbines at the ready, soldiers enter a cave while searching for a Taliban weapons cache in the Adi Ghar mountains, Afghanistan, in support of Operation Enduring Freedom.

RIGHT:

Sector of Fire

Soldiers with Charlie Company, 1st Battalion, 4th Infantry Regiment, discuss their sectors of fire during an area reconnaissance mission off Highway 1 in Zabul province, Afghanistan.

Giant Transporter
Soldiers from 12th Combat Aviation Brigade, out of Ansbach, Germany, offload an AH-64 Apache helicopter from a C5 Galaxy cargo aircraft in Mazar-i-Sharif, Afghanistan. The brigade was deploying to Afghanistan's Regional Command North in support of Operation Enduring Freedom.

Artillery Airlift
The load team hooks up an M777A2 howitzer to be airlifted from Forward Operating Base Hadrian to Kandahar Airfield by an Army CH-47 Chinook helicopter from Task Force Knighthawk. The Chinook is frequently used to transport personnel and material to the fight.

Medevac
A flight medic checks to ensure IV fluid is flowing properly to a wounded Afghan National Army soldier during a patient transfer mission at Forward Operating Base Tagab, Kapisa province, Afghanistan.

OPPOSITE:

Standing Watch

Soldiers with 1st Battalion, 6th Field Artillery Regiment, 3rd Brigade, 1st Infantry Division, Focused Targeting Force, stand watch while their unit boards a CH-47 Chinook helicopter in Khowst province, Afghanistan.

RIGHT:

Target Identification

A U.S. Army soldier with the Multi-Iraqi Transitional Team, 4th Battalion, 2nd Brigade, 5th Iraqi Army Division, uses the scope on his M4 carbine to identify and engage an enemy target during an operation in Buhriz, Iraq.

LEFT:
Cargo Transport
A soldier drives a light vehicle into a C-130 Hercules aircraft at Sather Air Base, Iraq. The C-130 is an American four-engine turboprop military transport capable of using unprepared runways for takeoffs and landings. The C-130 was originally designed as a troop, medevac, and cargo transport aircraft.

ABOVE:
Security Inspection
Soldiers from the 10th Mountain Division coordinate security points during an inspection of an Iraqi police checkpoint near Joint Site Security Shaura Um Jidr, Baghdad, Iraq. The inspection was regarding the installation of solar-powered lights to increase night time visibility.

Cordon and Search Operation
Armed with an M249 light machine gun, Spc. Brett Bell, a fire support specialist assigned to Echo Company, 2nd Battalion, 5th Cavalry Regiment, 1st Cavalry Division, searches for contacts from a covered position during a cordon and search operation in western Baghdad, Iraq.

ABOVE:

M1A2 Abrams Tanks on Patrol
Army M1A2 Abrams tanks patrol in the city of Tall Afar, Iraq. The M1 Abrams is a third-generation American main battle tank used for ground warfare and is one of the heaviest tanks in service at nearly 68 short tons (61.7 tonnes).

OPPOSITE:

Extraction Mission
Soldiers from the 101st Airborne Division run to UH-60 Black Hawk helicopters after conducting a search for weapons caches in Albu Issa, Iraq. The Black Hawk is frequently used for insertion and extraction of small units.

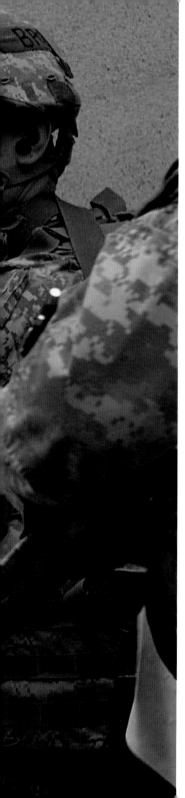

LEFT:

Street Clearing

Army Private Joseph Burton and Staff Sergeant John Martinez from the 1st Cavalry Division clear a street corner during a raid in the Tamooz neighborhood of Mosul, Iraq. Using a wall for cover, the soldiers prepare to turn the approaching corner.

ABOVE AND RIGHT:

Forward Observers

Army Pfc. Jason Dore (above) uses his binoculars to scan for any possible enemy contact in western Baghdad, Iraq. Dore was assigned as a forward observer with the 2nd Battalion, 5th Cavalry Regiment. Soldiers from the 1st Cavalry Division (right) scan for enemy snipers at the Nineveh ancient ruins in Mosul, Iraq. Snipers could be anywhere, so the soldiers use their scopes from covered positions to spot enemies while remaining hidden.

ABOVE:
Joint Clearing Operation
A Bradley infantry fighting vehicle provides security as soldiers from the 3rd Infantry Division conduct a joint clearing operation with local Abna'a Al Iraq (Sons of Iraq) through a group of small villages south of Salman Pak, Iraq. The village was known to have harbored insurgents.

RIGHT:
Car Bomb
In south Baghdad, an explosion goes off from a second car bomb aimed at U.S. and Iraqi forces arriving to inspect the first car bomb detonated an hour earlier. The original target was the local Iraqi police force. Of the 18 casualties, only two were police officers.

LEFT:

Dismounted Patrol
Paratroopers with the 319th Airborne Field Artillery Regiment, 82nd Airborne Division, conduct a dismounted patrol through Al Suleikh, Iraq. A dismounted patrol is a foot patrol, in this case, along a well-covered road.

OPPOSITE:

MLRS Practice Rocket
A precision-guided missile is fired near Tikrit, Iraq. The multiple launch rocket system (MLRS) is a high-mobility automatic system based on the M270 weapons platform. The crew of three (driver, gunner, and section chief) can fire up to 12 rockets in less than a minute without leaving the cab of the vehicle.

OPPOSITE:

M1A2 Training

An M1A2 Abrams tank maneuvers during a platoon live-fire exercise as part of Agile Spirit 19 at Orpholo Training Area, Georgia. AgS19 ensures that U.S., allied, and partnered nations maintain a conventional deterrence capability with a combination of combat-ready forward forces.

ABOVE:

Helping a Comrade

Climbing a hill while on patrol. Pfc. Ryan Mahan extends a hand to help Spc. Stephen McLain up a hill in Chinchal, Iraq. The soldiers are assigned to 1st Brigade Combat Team, 10th Mountain Division.

RIGHT:

Metal Detector

A paratrooper with the 505th Parachute Infantry Regiment uses a metal detector in search of a weapons cache during Operation Doubleday in the New Baghdad district of eastern Baghdad. The combined clearance operation was conducted to disrupt insurgent networks.

M119 Howitzer
Soldiers with Alpha Battery,
3rd Battalion, 7th Field
Artillery Regiment, fire an
M119 light howitzer during a
live-fire exercise near Kirkuk,
Iraq. The M119 can be easily
airlifted by helicopter, or
dropped by parachute.

LEFT:
Joint Operation
CH-47 Chinook helicopters land outside of the village of Abd al Hasan, Iraq, to take U.S. and Iraqi Army soldiers back to Forward Operating Base McHenry, after the completion of a combat operation. During the operation, the soldiers delivered humanitarian relief supplies and searched houses to clear the area for future operations.

BELOW:
Ground Support Mission
An OH-58 Kiowa helicopter from the 25th Combat Aviation Brigade (CAB) flies a mission in the area of Kirkuk, Iraq. During their deployment, the 25th CAB provided air support for ground forces. This OH-58 is armed with Hellfire missiles, a 100lb (45kg) air-to-ground precision weapon designed to destroy high-value targets.

LEFT:

Convoy Protection

Army Staff Sergeant Harvey scans the horizon through the scope of his M4 carbine after taking sniper fire in Dhi Qar province, Iraq. Soldiers of the 77th Armored Regiment were on a convoy mission when they were hit by sniper fire.

RIGHT:

Search and Destroy Mission

Soldiers from the 101st Airborne Division and Iraqi Army search for a weapons cache on a farm outside of Hawijah, Iraq. The soldiers were attached to Alpha Company, 1st Battalion, 327th Infantry Regiment.

ALL PHOTOGRAPHS:
Mounted Patrols
Pictured left, Spc. Christopher Newell, a turret gunner with 152nd Cavalry Regiment, prepares to go out on a mounted patrol in a Mine Resistant Ambush Protected (MRAP) vehicle after conducting pre-combat inspections and checks.

Pictured right, Pfc. John Courson, from Charlie Company, 2nd Battalion, 1st Brigade, 101st Airborne Division, stands before a convoy of armored vehicles operated by his unit.

ABOVE:

Medical Mission

Spc. Deidre Olivas from the 7th Cavalry Regiment makes an Iraqi child's day by presenting her with a stuffed animal. The child was waiting for medical treatment and Olivas was working as part of a combined medical mission in Quadria, Iraq.

OPPOSITE:

Working Dog

U.S. Army Staff Sergeant Kevin Reese from the 2nd Infantry Division and his military working dog Grek wait at a safe house before conducting an assault against insurgents in Buhriz, Iraq.

RIGHT TOP:

History Lesson

Taken in 2007, Pfc. Rebekah Yokel from the 82nd Airborne Division talks with a young Iraqi girl during a visit by Iraqi nationals to the historic Ziggurat of Ur, located near Imam Ali Air Base, Iraq. This was the first time in 10 years that civilians had been allowed to step on the grounds of the historic site, which was built in the ancient city of Ur and includes the house of the biblical prophet Abraham.

RIGHT BELOW:

Community Relations

First Lieutenant Eric Gianneris meets a local shop owner while conducting a joint patrol in Shulla, Iraq. Conducting community relations with locals is crucial in demonstrating that American soldiers are there to help.

Tactical Checkpoint

Spc. Jarrod MacEachern from the 25th Infantry Division provides on-the-ground security while conducting a tactical checkpoint near Patrol Base Doria, Iraq. Tactical checkpoints exist to limit the movement of insurgents in contested areas.

M21 Sniper Weapon System (SWS)

Sergeant Eddi Mathis holds his 7.62mm M21 sniper rifle at ready while pulling security during a dismounted patrol in Balad Ruz, Iraq. Prized for its durability and accuracy, the M21 is a Vietnam War-era rifle that came back into favor.

Convoy Stop

A soldier with the 82nd Airborne Division rests on the dropdown stairs of his Mine Resistant Ambush Protected (MRAP) vehicle while crossing the border from Iraq into neighboring Kuwait.

Street Patrol

Spc. Carlos Santos surveys the streets of Jamia, Iraq, for insurgent activity. Santos is assigned to Camp Liberty in Baghdad, Iraq, which was used from 2012 to 2016 to house members of the People's Mujahedin of Iran.

LEFT:
Simulated Chemical Attack
A soldier calls in a medical evacuation after a simulated chemical attack during a training mission near Camp Ramadi, Iraq. All members of the training mission wear gasmasks, which would be required if such an attack ocurred.

OPPOSITE:
Run-Up
Major Robert Kneeland (right), the commanding officer of the 45th Medical Company (Air Ambulance), and Chief Warrant Officer Kevin W. Jordan, prepare to do a run-up on a UH-60A Black Hawk helicopter at Al Asad Air Base, Iraq. Run-ups are done to ensure that all equipment and the helicopter itself are properly working before conducting missions.

OPPOSITE:

Armored Deployment, South Korea

M1 Abrams tanks from the 1st Armored Brigade Combat Team, 3rd Infantry Division, train at Rodriguez Live Fire Complex, South Korea. The Raider Brigade is in Korea as the rotational tank brigade supporting the U.S. 2nd Infantry Division.

LEFT:

Patrolling the Demilitarized Zone (DMZ), Korea

South Korean and American soldiers patrol along a fence at the United Nations Security Area in Panmunjom, during an annual training exercise. Panmunjom is where the Korean War armistice was signed in 1953. It is estimated that roughly 18,000 U.S. Army troops were stationed in Korea in 2020, helping ensure that peace is maintained between North and South Korea.

OPPOSITE:
Joint Security Area, DMZ, Korea
South Korean and U.S. soldiers of the Neutral Surveillance Mission stand by the blue barracks at the Demilitarized Zone (DMZ) in Panmunjom, Korea. In the distance soldiers of the North Korean People's Army can be seen.

RIGHT:
Marksman Training
Sergeant James Balestrini takes up a prone position to qualify on the M240/249 Montana Range in South Korea. The objectives of machine gun marksmanship training are to produce gunners that are thoroughly capable of demonstrating an accurate initial burst, adjusting fire, and firing at speed.

OVERLEAF:
Paladin Self-propelled Guns, Topyong-Ri, South Korea
Soldiers from Battery B, 1st Battalion, 82nd Field Artillery Regiment, 1st Cavalry Division, fire 155mm (6.1in) shells from a battery of M109A6 Paladin howitzers at the Nightmare Range target practice area, July 2020.

Picture Credits

Airsealand.Photos: 41, 43 left, 44 both, 48, 57 bottom, 80–86 all

Alamy: 32/33 & 49 (Everett Collection), 51 (Granger Historical Archive), 88 (Dino Fracchia), 219 (Everett Collection), 220 (Sueddeutsche Zeitung)

Getty Images: 45 (Underwood Collection), 53 (Umberto Cicconi), 58 (Bettmann), 70 (Popperfoto), 76 (ullstein bild), 77 (Corbis), 78 (Keystone), 79 (Hulton), 87 (Spec 4 Peter Finnegan/US Army/PhotoQuest), 89 (Manoocher Deghati), 90 (Tom Stoddart Archive), 91 (Gerard Fouet), 92 (Eric Bouvet), 93 left (Kevin Weaver), 93 right (Mike Nelson), 94 (Leif Skoogfors), 95 (Tarik Rinazay)

Library of Congress: 24, 26, 27, 43 right

National Archives and Records Administration: 28–31 all, 34–39 all, 42, 50 both, 52, 54–57 top, 59–69 all, 72–75 all

New Jersey National Guard/Mark C Olsen: 16 bottom left, 101, 105, 167

Oregon National Guard: 104 (SFC April Davis)

South Carolina National Guard: 158 (Sgt Jorge Intriago)

U.S. Air Force: 15 top right (SSG Shawn White), 18 (SrA Dilia DeGrego), 19 left (A1C Theodore J Koniares), 111 left (SrA Joshua Strang), 162 (Capt Tony Vincelli), 175 (SrA Sean Martin), 187 (SSG Stacy L Pearsall), 188 (TSG Jeffrey Allen), 194 & 195 right (SSG Vanessa Valentine), 202/203 & 204 (SSG Dallas Edwards), 210 (SSG Stacy L Pearsall), 211 left (TSG William Greer), 211 top right (MSG Robert W Valenca), 212 (MSG Andy Dunaway), 213 (SSG Shane A Cuomo), 215 (MSG Brian L Boone)

U.S. Air National Guard: 96 (TSG Sarah Mattison)

U.S. Army: 9, 10 top (Spc Joshua Edwards), 10 bottom, 11 (Spc Katelyn Strange), 12/13 (SSG Teddy Wade), 14 (SSG Ali E Flisek), 15 left (SSG Jason Epperson), 15 bottom right (SSG Christopher Marasky), 16 top left (Sgt Gregory Williams), 16 right (Jason Johnston), 17 (SSG Crista Yazzie), 19 right (Pfc Andrya Hill), 20 (Gertrud Zach), 21 (Spc Venessa Hernandez), 22 (Robert Shields), 23 (Tommy Gilligan), 98 left (SSG Russell Lee Klika), 98 right (John D Helms), 99 (Sgt Keith Rogers), 100 (Winifred Brown), 102 left (Sgt Brandon Bolick), 102 right (Sgt Richard Wrigley), 103 (Patrick A Albright), 106 (Luis Viegas), 107 (Gertrud Zach), 108 (SSG Lonnie Woods) 109 (Sgt Sean Mathis), 110 (Jason W Edwards), 111 right (Sgt Brady Pritchett), 112 (Paolo Bovo), 113 (Gertrud Zach), 114 (Paolo Bovo), 115 top left (Fred W Baker III), 115 bottom left (SSG Bryan Dominique), 115 right, 116 (SSG Chrissy Best), 117 (SSG Pablo N Piedra), 118 (Spc Joshua Edwards), 119 (MSG Michel Sauret), 120 (Maj Bruce Roberts), 121 (Abigail Meyer), 122 (SSG Mark Patton), 123 (John D Helms), 124 (Sgt Christopher Prows), 125 (Sgt Bryanna Poulin), 126/127 (SSG David Hamann), 128 (Sgt Jennifer Lena), 129, 130 (Sgt Alexandra Hulett), 131 (Patrick A Albright), 132 (PFC Michael Bradley), 133 (Sgt Alexandra Hulett), 134 (Phil Manson), 135 (SSG Russell Lee Klika), 136/137 (Sgt Emily Finn), 138 (Sgt Michael J MacLeod), 140 (Pvt Laurie Ellen Schubert), 141 (Spc Erik Anderson), 142 (Sgt Mason Cutrer), 143 (Spc Erik Anderson), 144 (SSG Pablo Piedra), 145 (Spc Hubert Delany), 146 (TSG Michael R Holzworth), 147 (Cpl Alisha Grezlik), 148 (Lt Col Deanna Bague), 149, 150 (SSG Jason Hull), 151 (Maj Randall Stillinger), 152 (SSG Andrew Smith), 153 left (PFC Nathaniel Newkirk), 153 right, 155 (Sgt Liane Hatch), 156 (Sgt Teddy Wade), 157 (TSG Joseph Prouse), 159 (SFC Brian Hamilton), 160 (Maj Anthony Chenault), 161 left (SFC John Laughter), 161 top right (1st Lt Miranda Summers Lowe), 161 bottom right (Spc Deomontez Duncan), 163 (Spc Michael J MacLeod), 164 (Calvin Reimold), 165 (Gertrud Zach), 166 (Spc Matthew A Thompson), 168 (Gary L Kieffer), 169 (Neysa Canfield), 170 (SSG Michael L Casteel), 172 (SSG Andrew Smith), 173 (Cpl Bertha A Flores), 174 (SSG Gary A Witte), 176 left (Sgt Teddy Wade), 176 right (Pfc Melissa M Escobar), 177 (TSG Francisco V Govea II), 178 (Spc Jacob Kohrs), 179 (Sgt Brandon Aird), 180 (SSG Leopold Medina, Jr), 181 (Spc Joshua Grenier), 182 (Major John C Crotzer), 184/185 (Sgt Duncan Brennan), 186 (PFC Donald Watkins), 189 (SPC Jesse Gross), 192 (SSG Aaron Allmon), 193 (Spc Luke Thornberry), 196 (Sgt Timothy Kingston), 197 (Spc Ronald Shaw Jr), 198 (Sgt Jeffrey Alexander), 199 (Spc Alisan Gul), 201 left (Spc Laura M Buchta), 206 (Spc Robert Sheets), 207 (Spc Timothy Kingston), 209 (Spc Jordan Huettl), 211 bottom right (Spc Charles Gill), 214 (SSG Lynette Hoke), 218 (Maj Peter Bogart), 221 (Sgt Alon Humphrey), 222/223 (Capt John DePinto)

U.S. Army National Guard: 154 (Sgt Heidi Kroll)

U.S. Department of Defense: 6 (Spc Ryan Lucas), 8 (Cherie A Thurlby), 46, 183 (OR-6 Mark Doran), 200 (SSG True Thao), 201 right (Spc Joshua W Lowery), 205 (Spc Bryanna Poulin), 208 (SSG James E Brown)

U.S. Marine Corps: 216 (Sgt Andrew D Pendracki), 217 (Sgt Maryalice Leone)

U.S. Navy: 190/191 & 195 left (MC2 Kitt Amaritnant)